TODDLER COLORING BOOK
FUNNY TIME TO LEARN

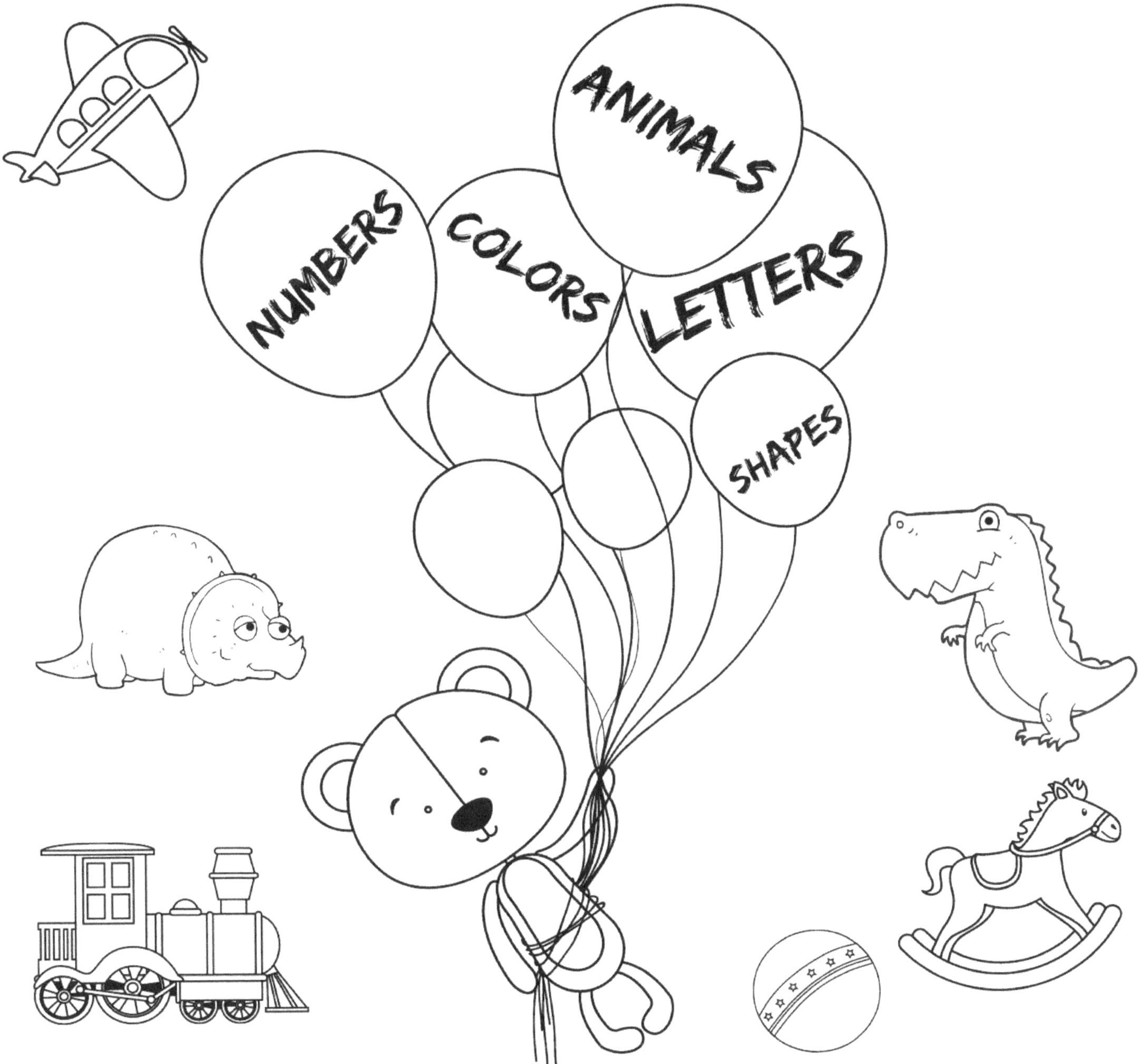

THIS
BOOK
BELONGS
TO :

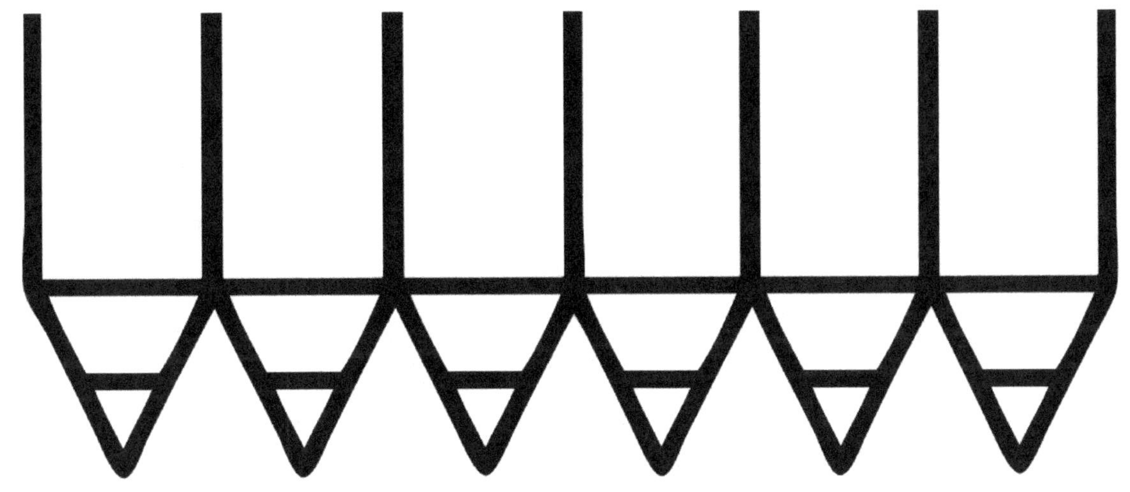

NUMBERS

1

ONE

2

TWO

THREE

FOUR

5

FIVE

6

SIX

7
SEVEN

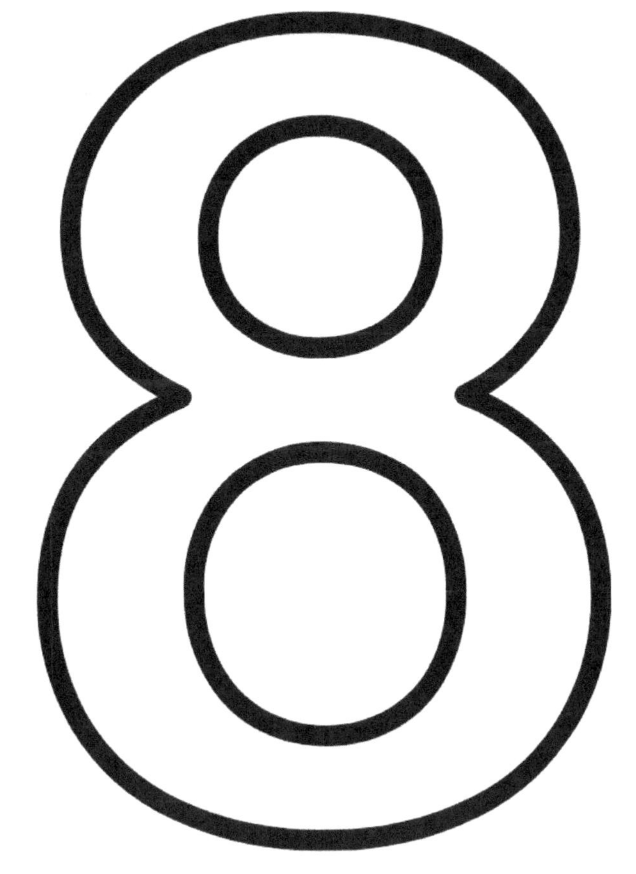

EIGHT

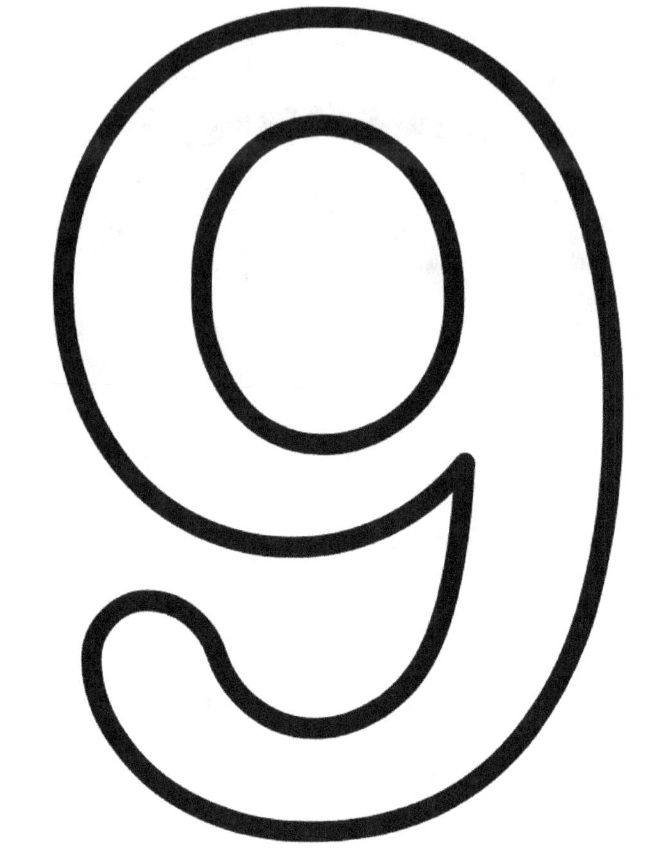

NINE

10

TEN

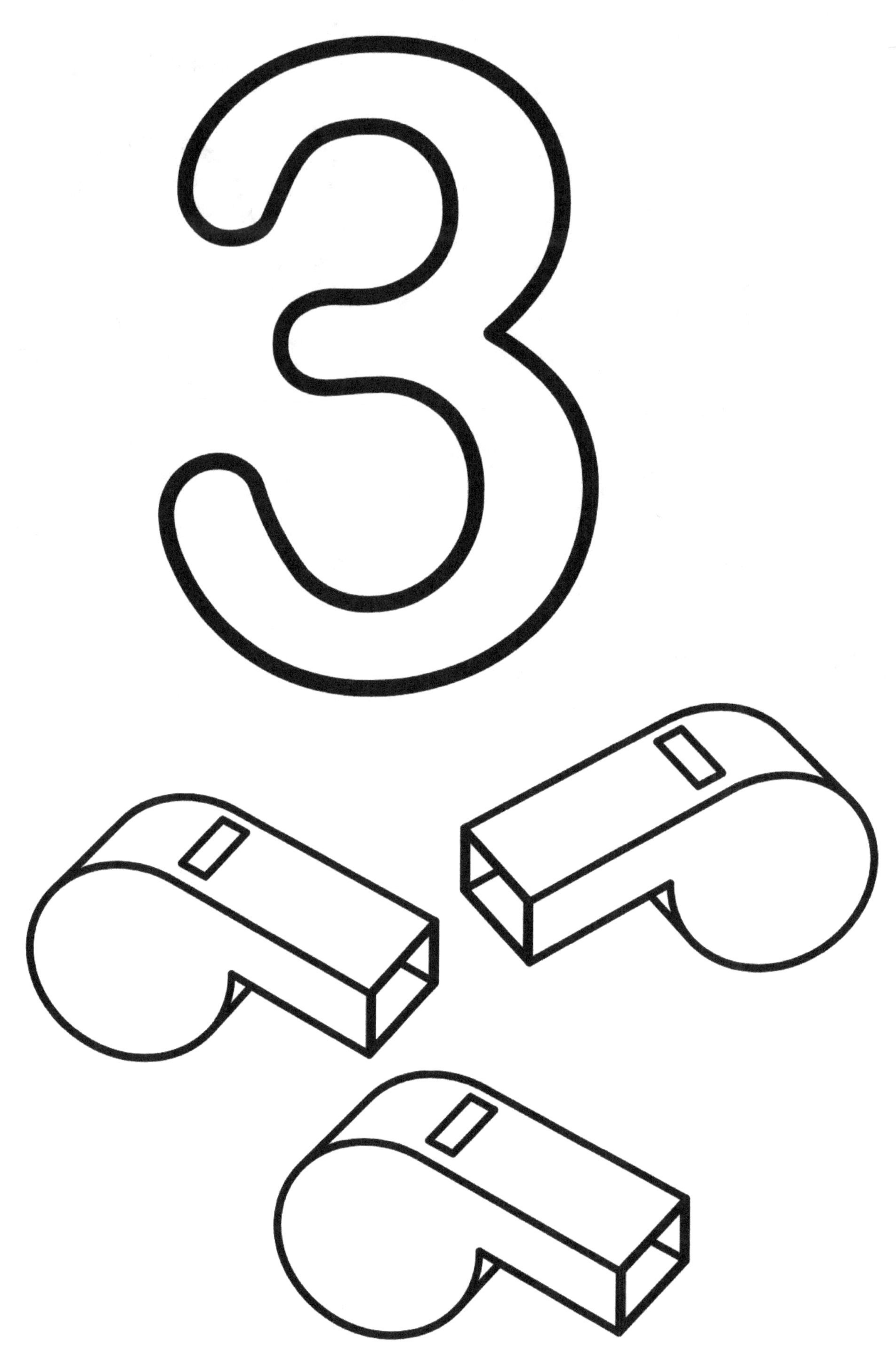

5

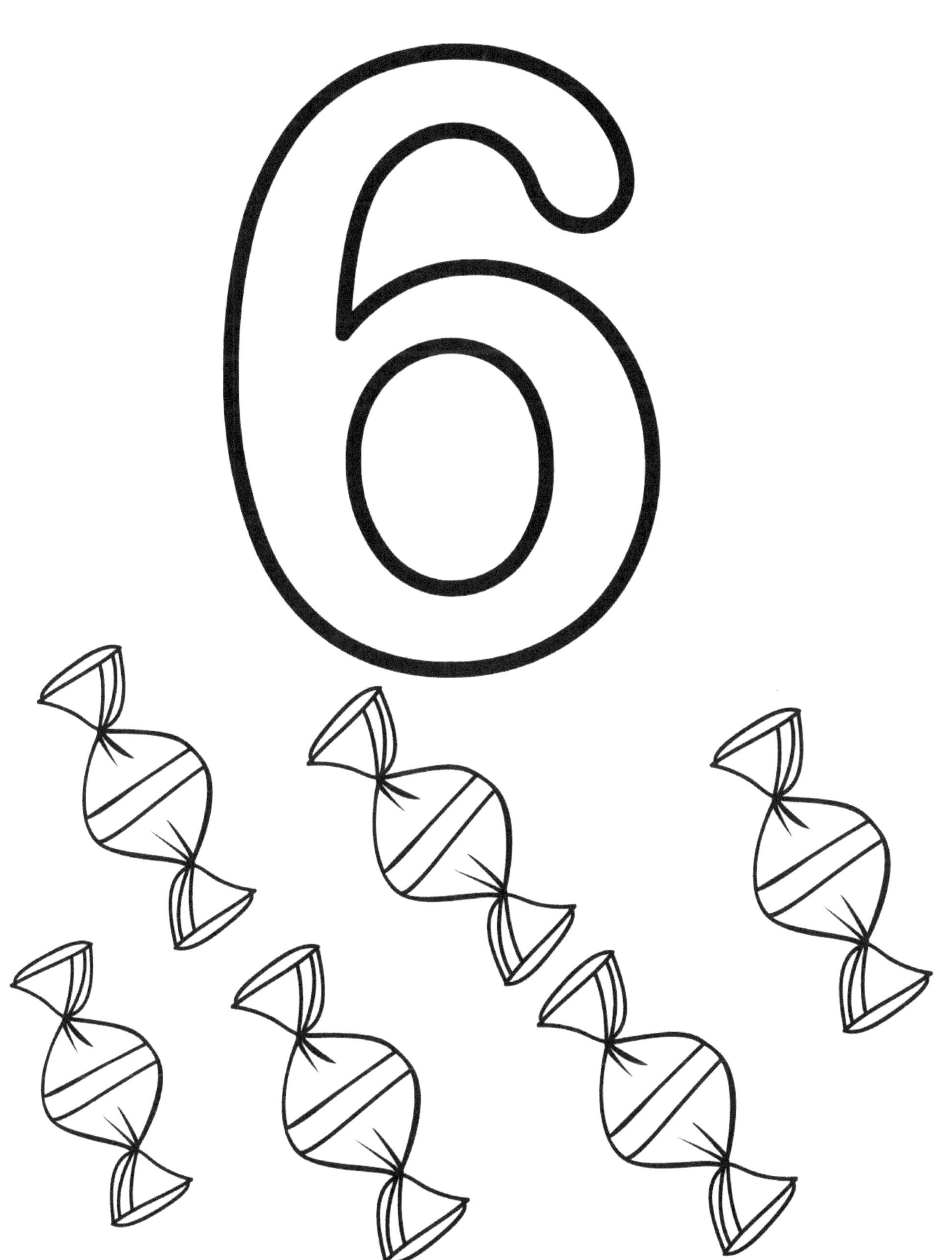

10

THE LETTERS

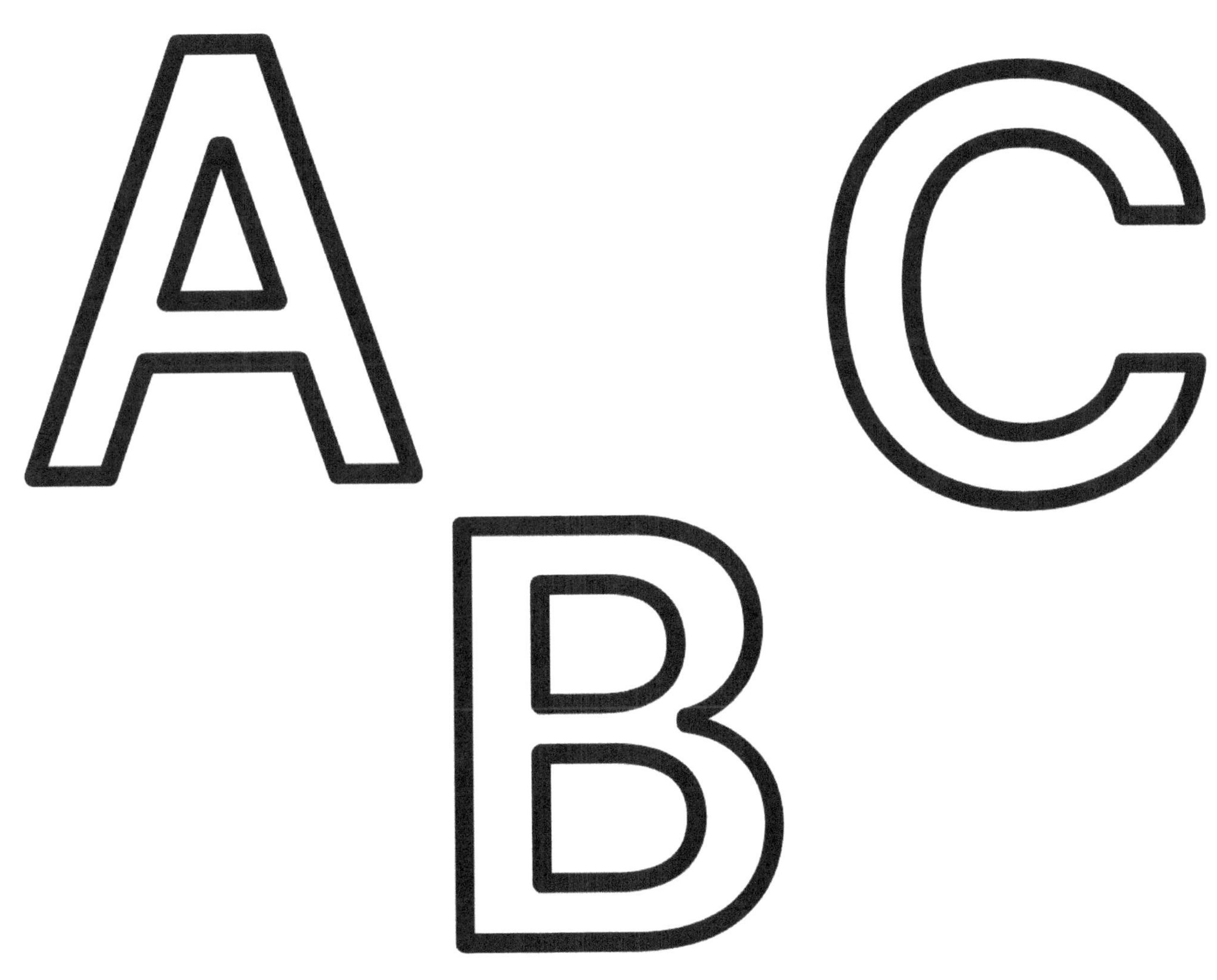

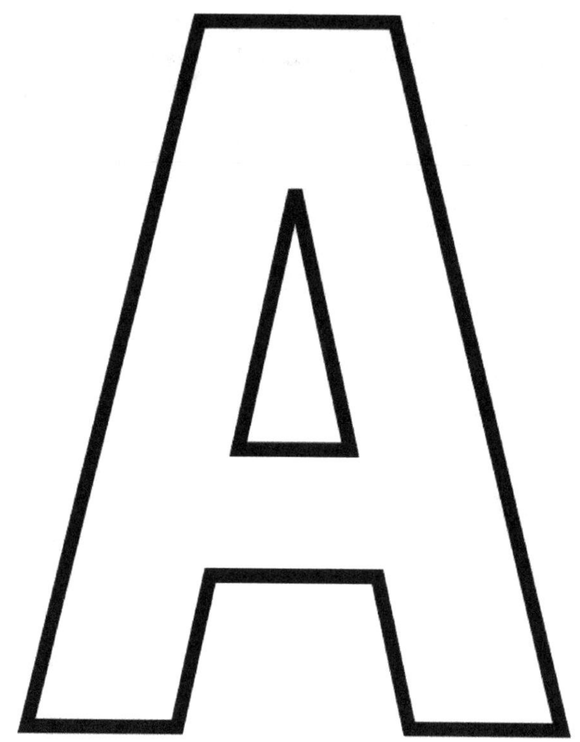

A a

APPLE

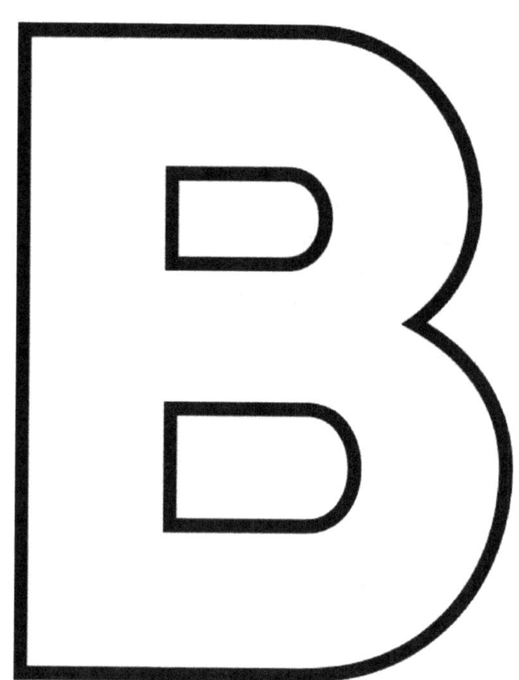

B b
banana

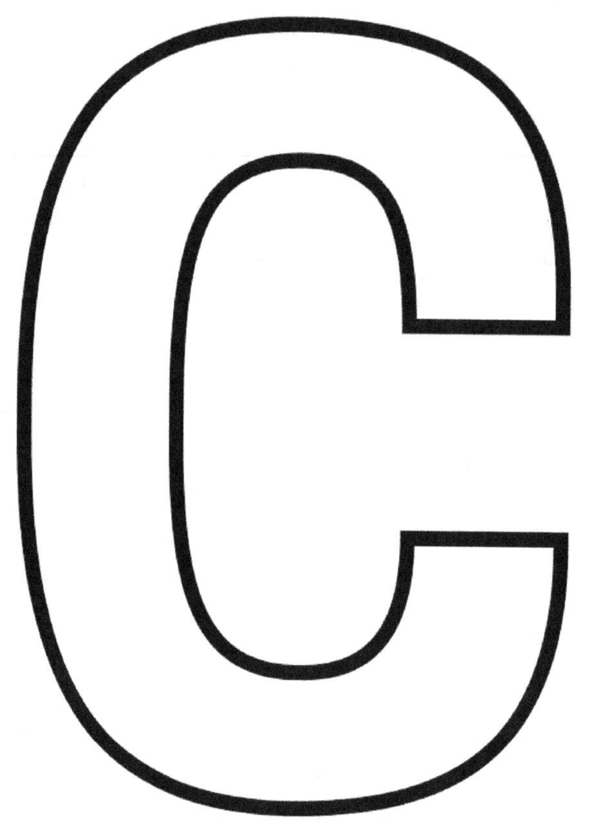

C c

carrot

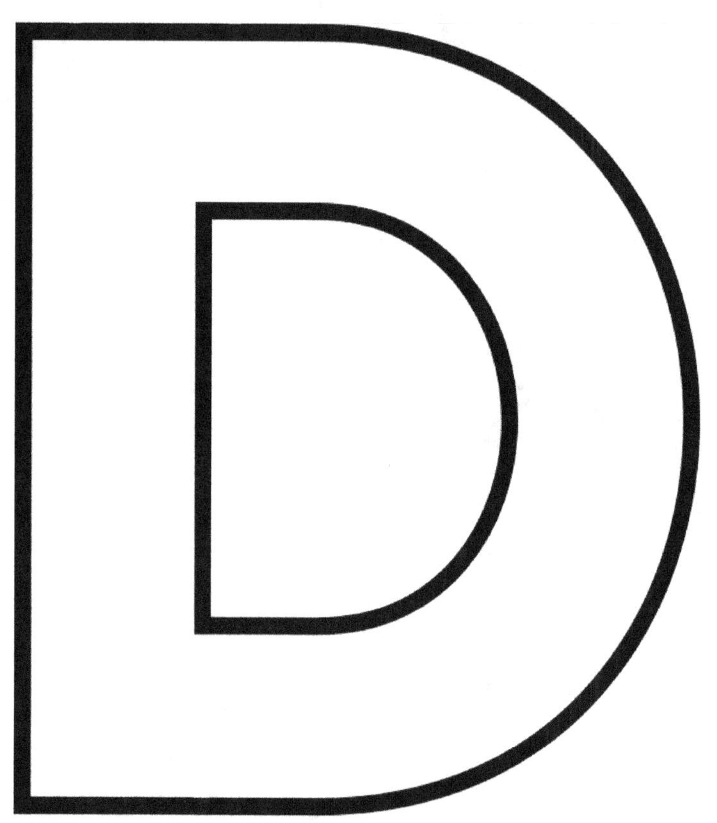

D d

Dinosaur

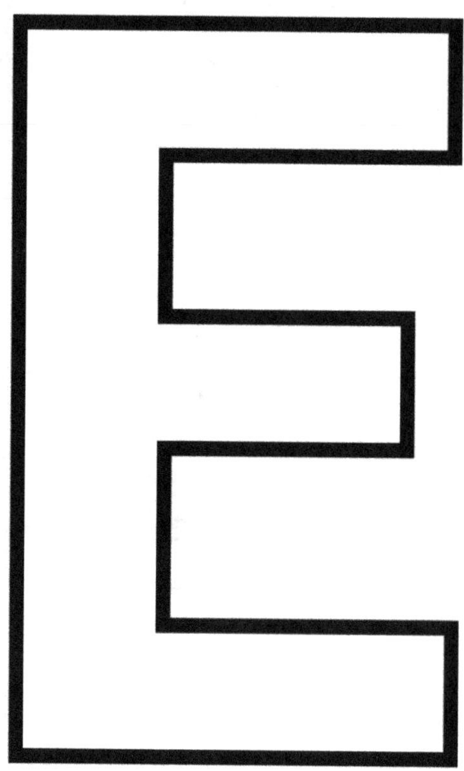

E e

elephant

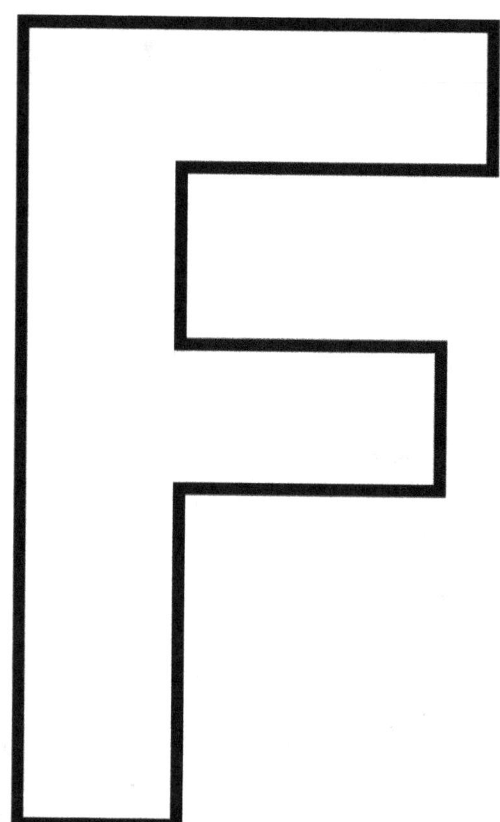

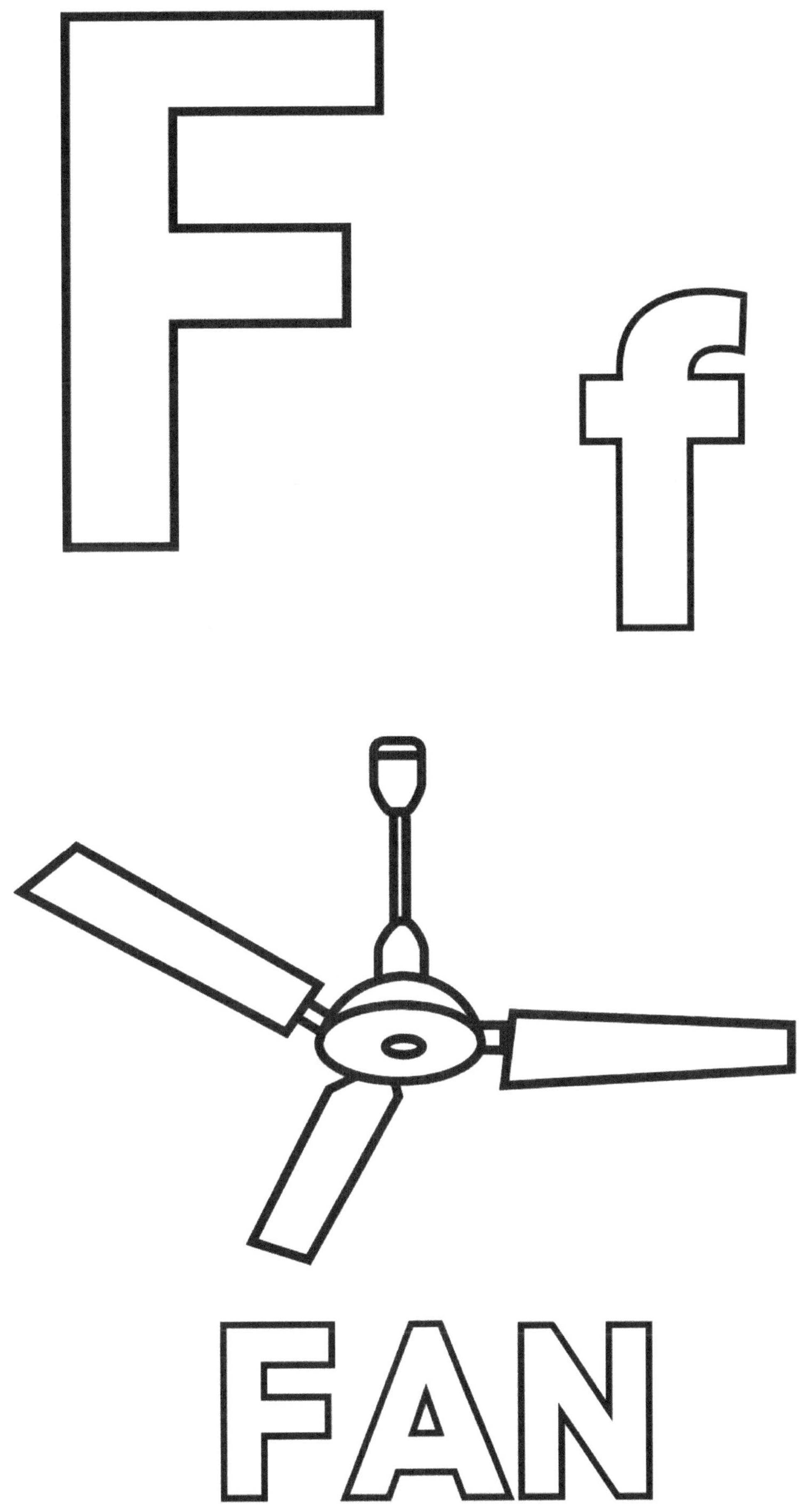

F f
FAN

G g

Grapes

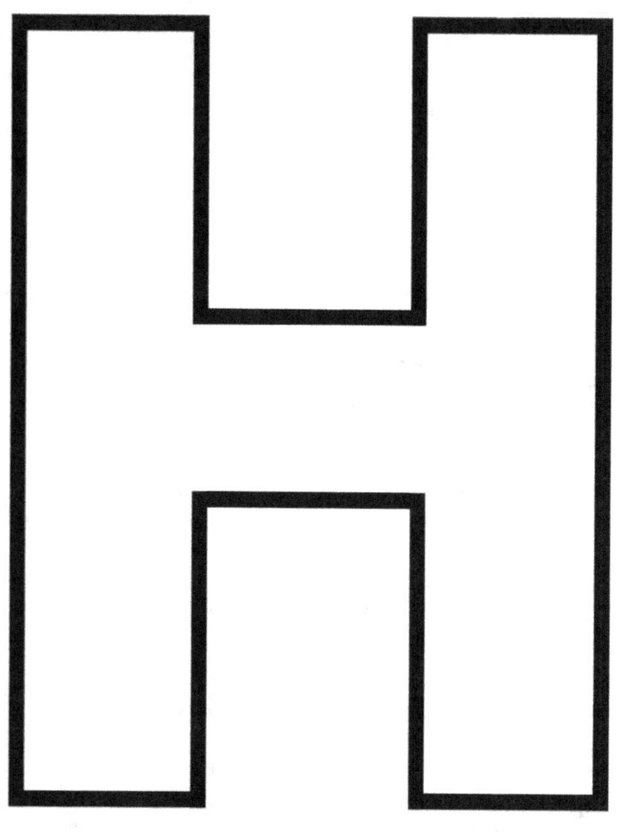

H h

hat

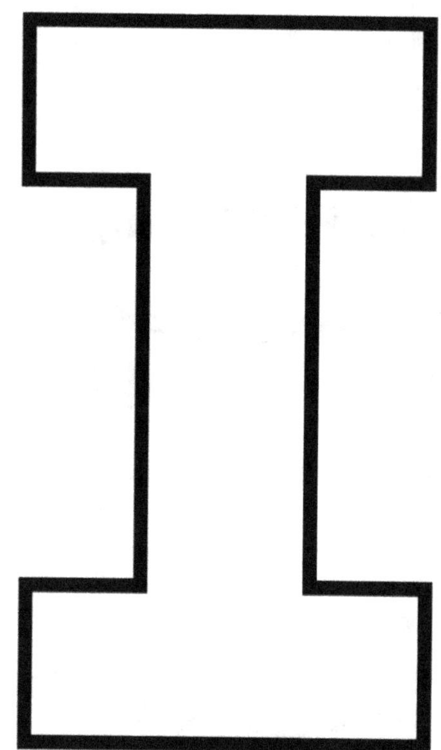

I i

insect

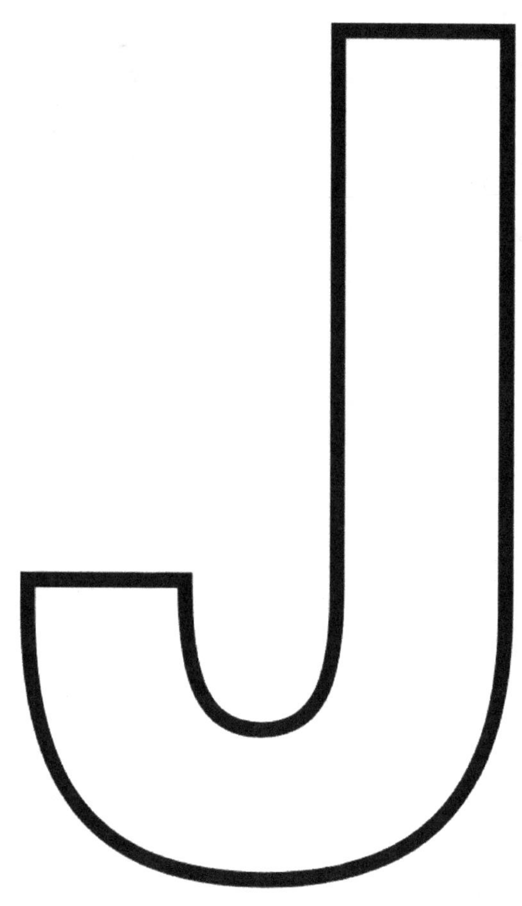

J j

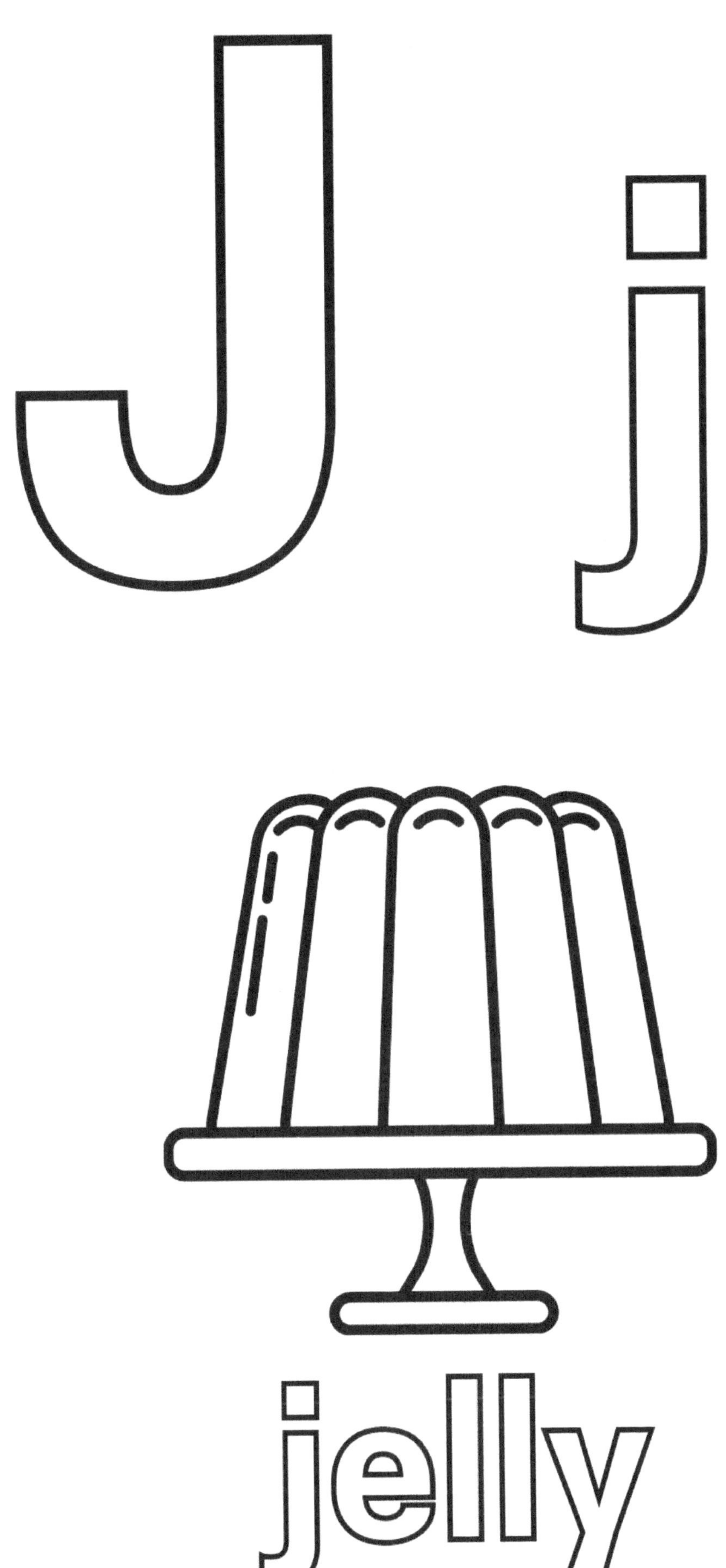

jelly

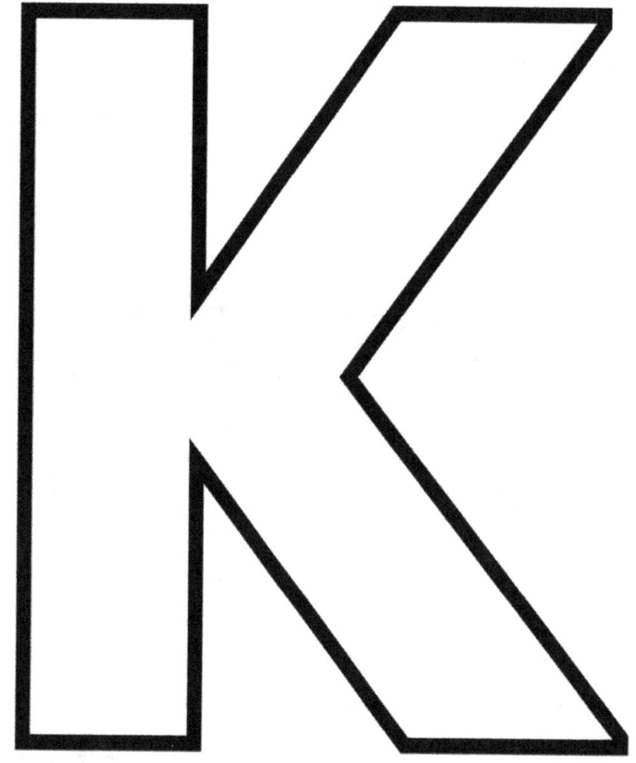

K k
key
kite

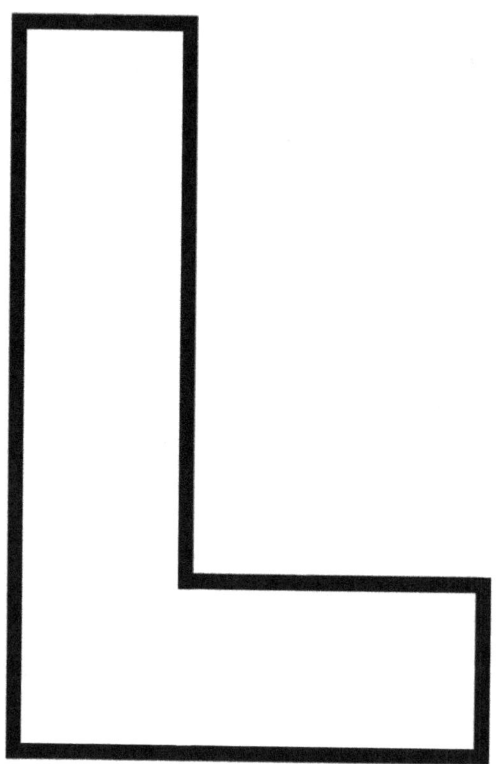

L l

M

M m
moon
mango

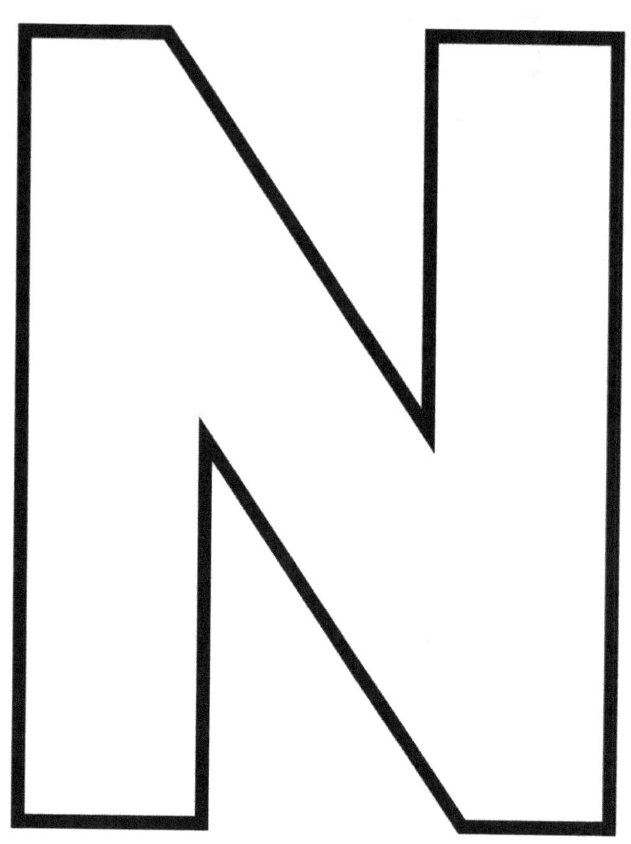

N n
Nose
Necklace

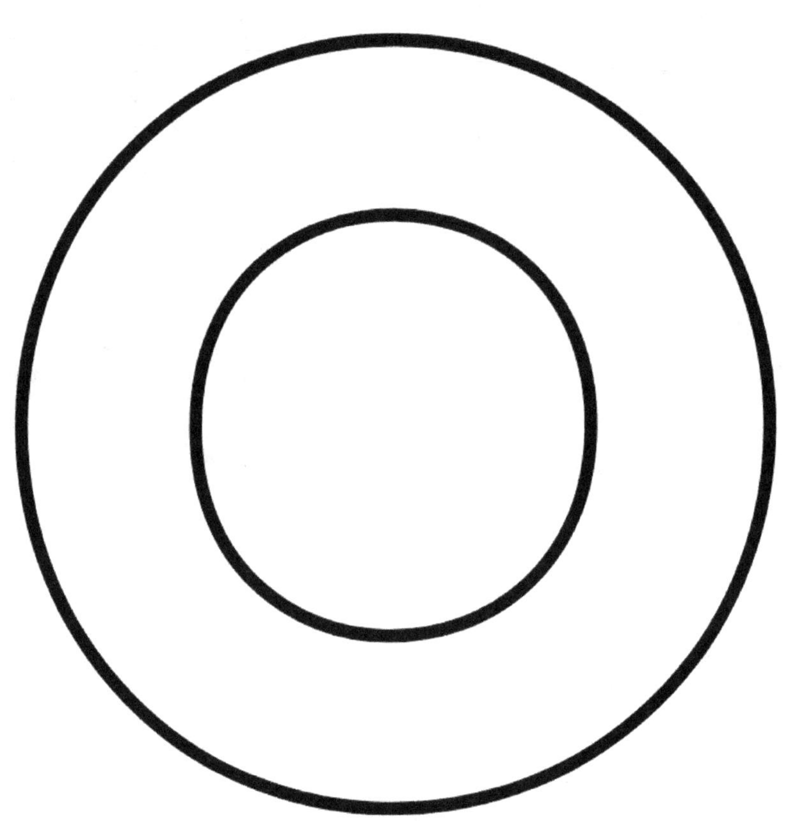

orange
oboe

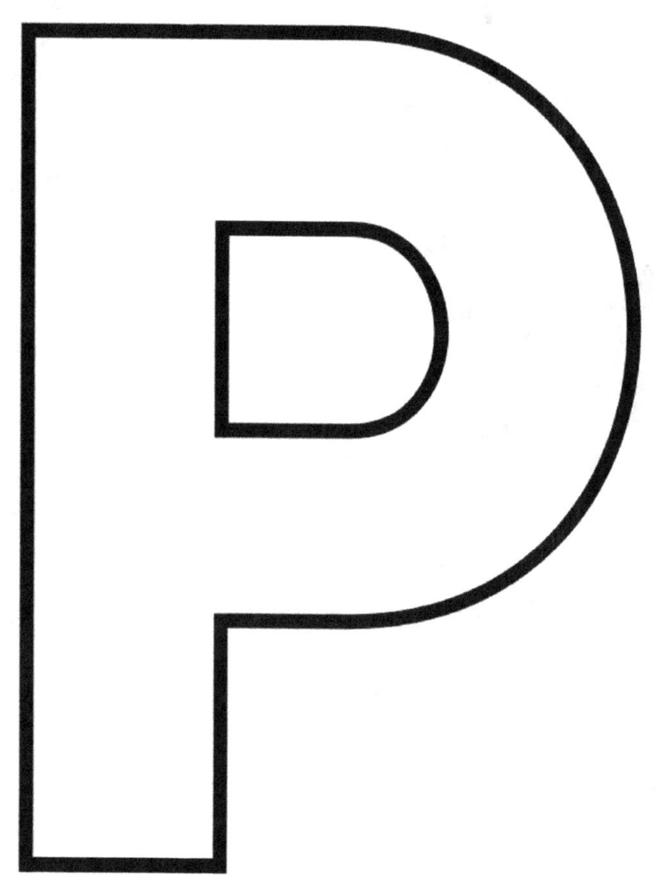

P p
pineapple
plant

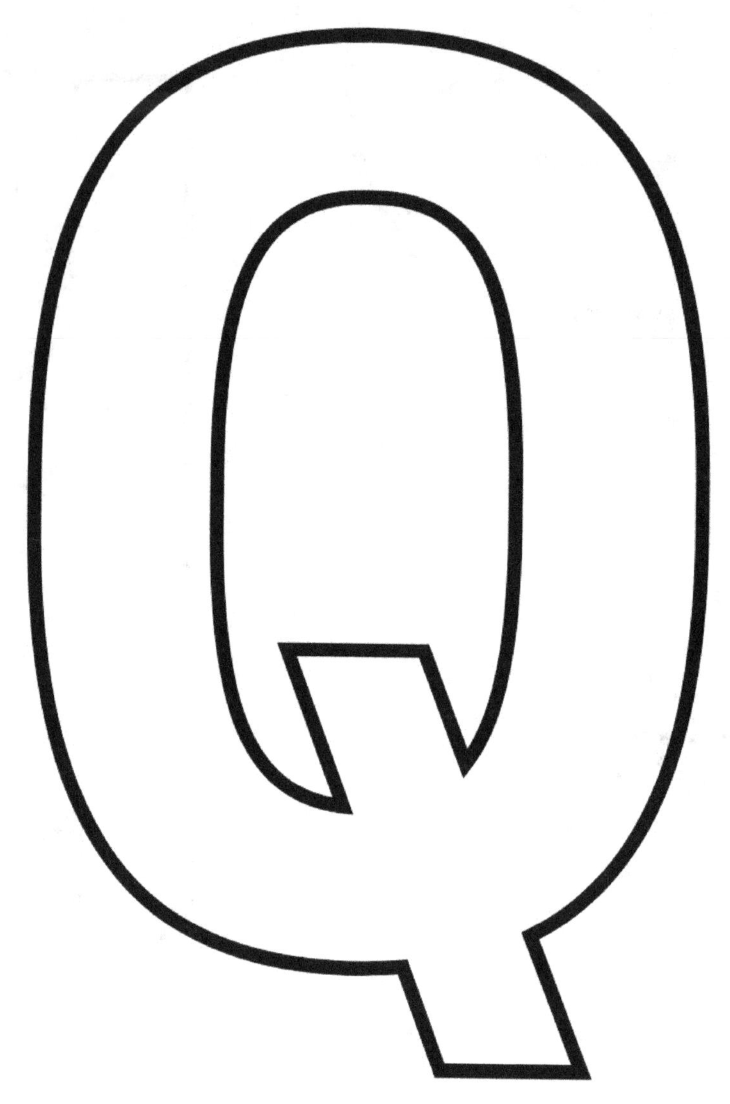

queen   quince

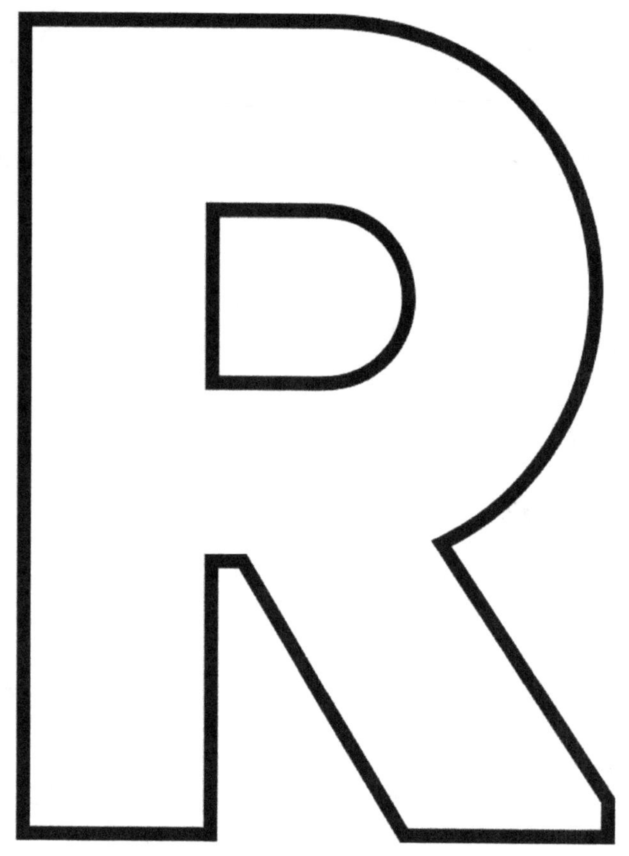

R r

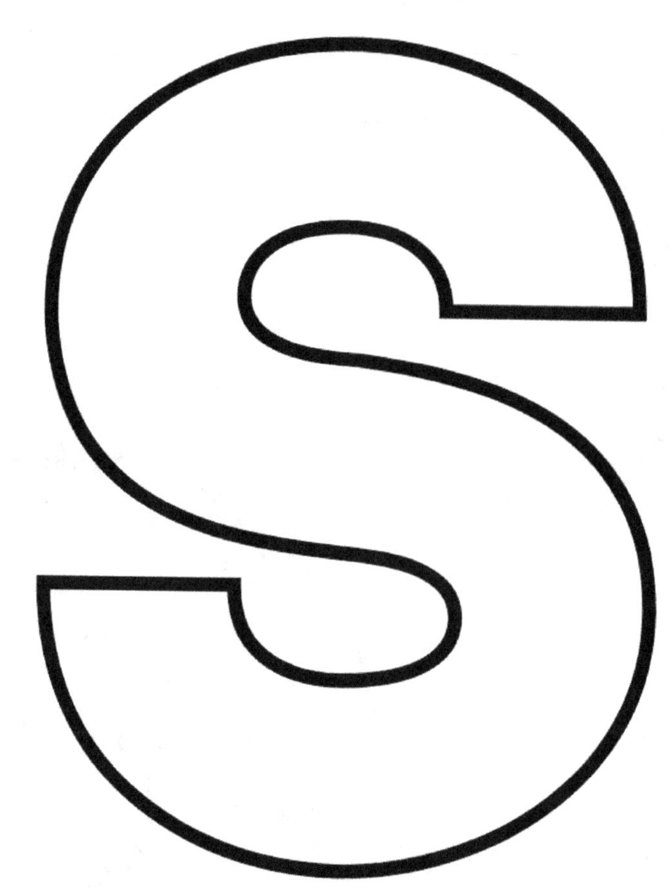

S s

T t
tomato
teddy

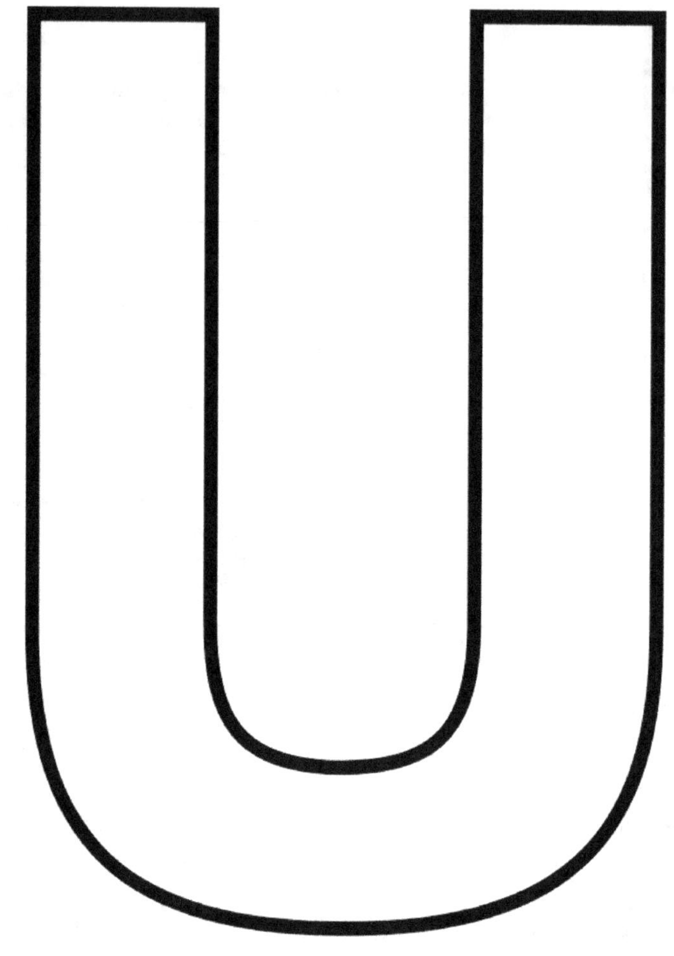

Uu

umbrella

unicorn

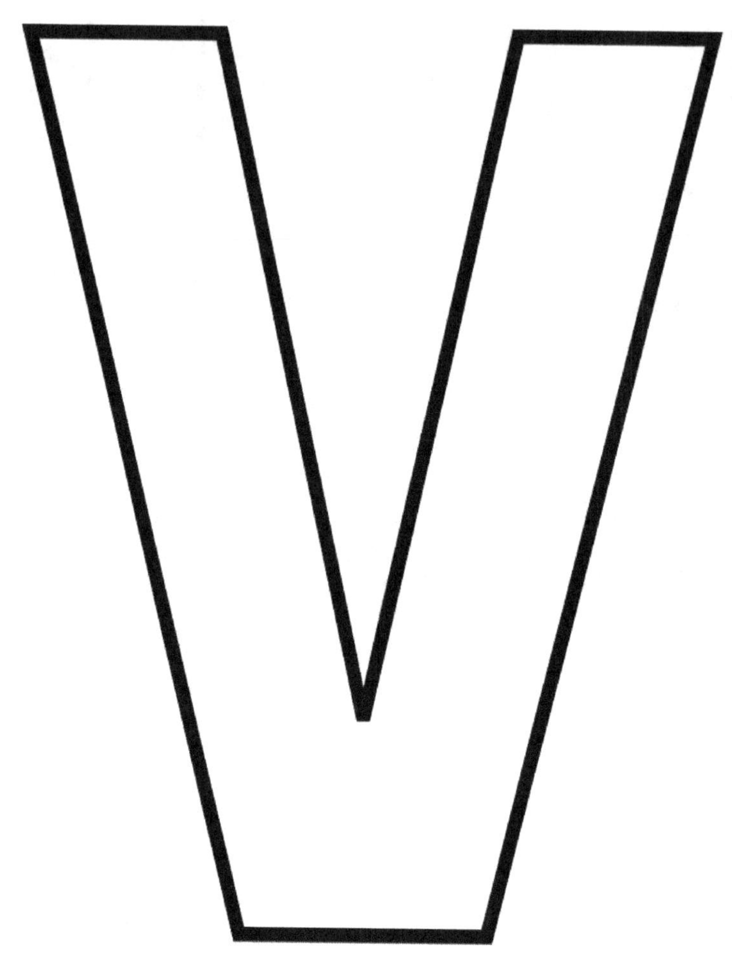

V v
violin
vase

W w

watermelon

window

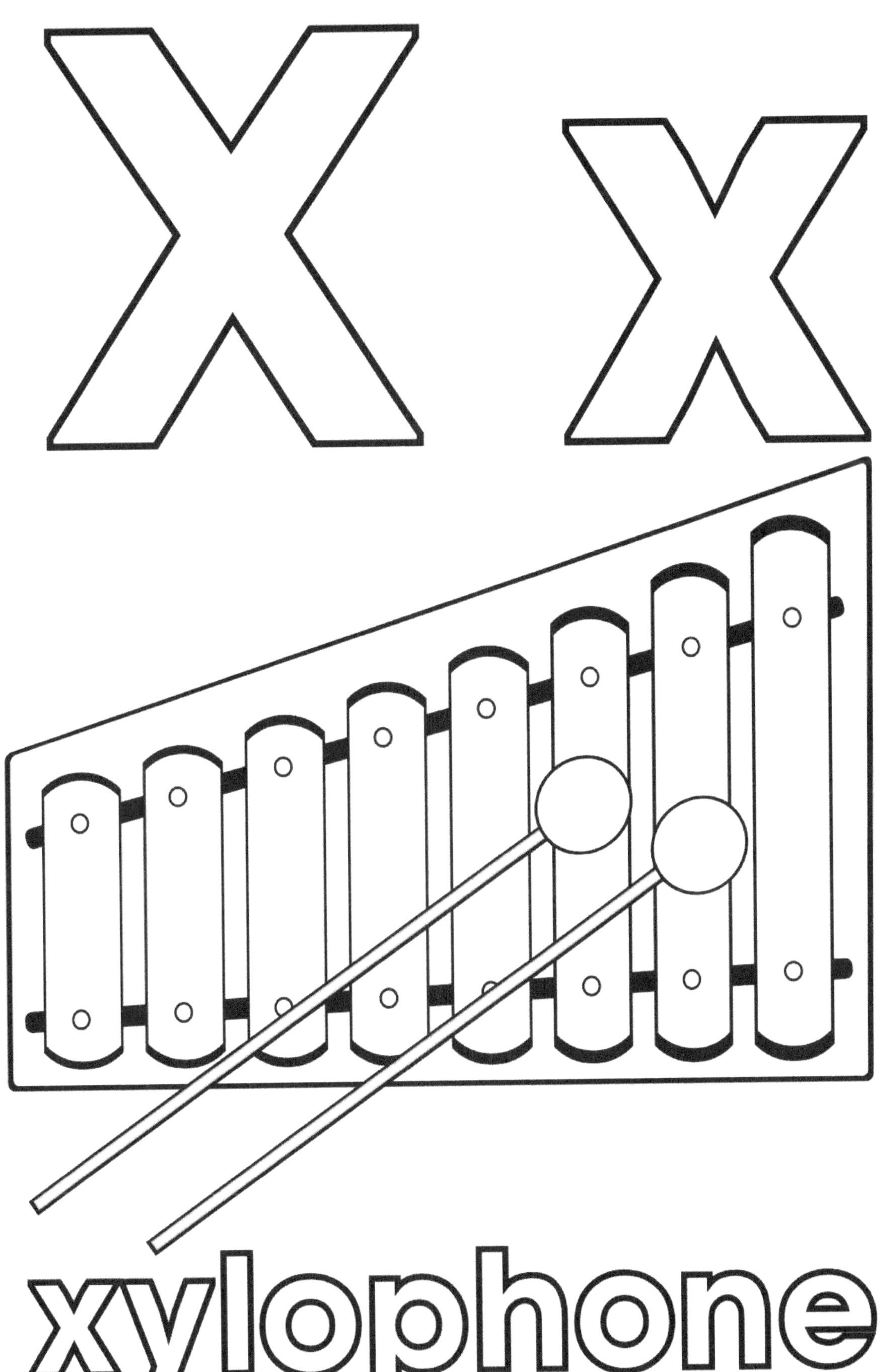

X x
xylophone

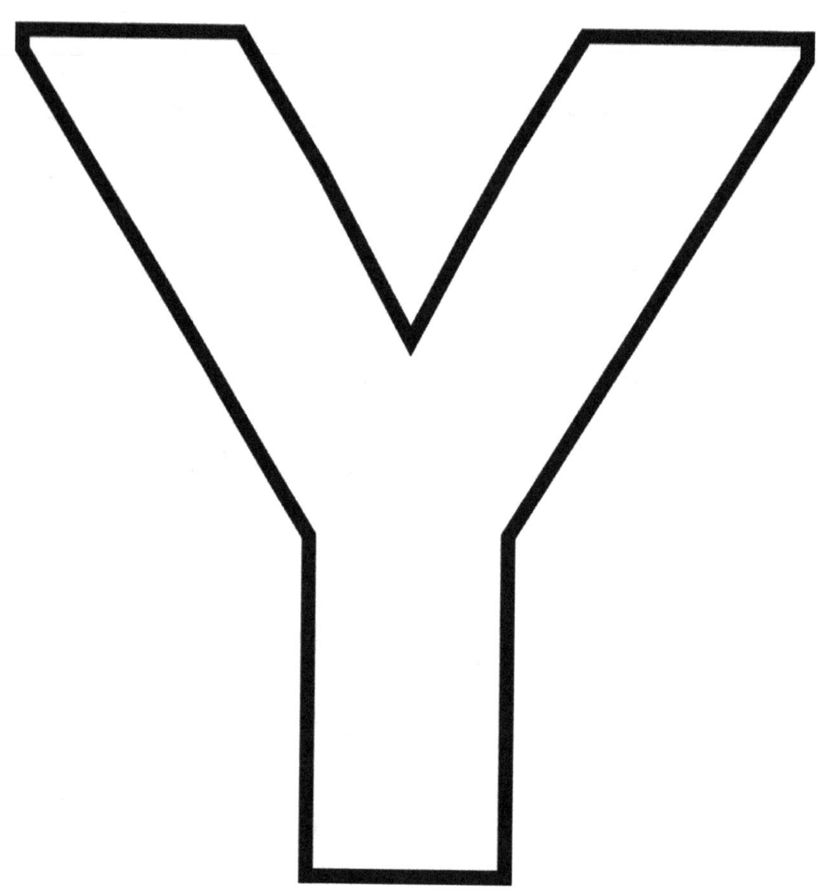

Y y
yolk   yoyo

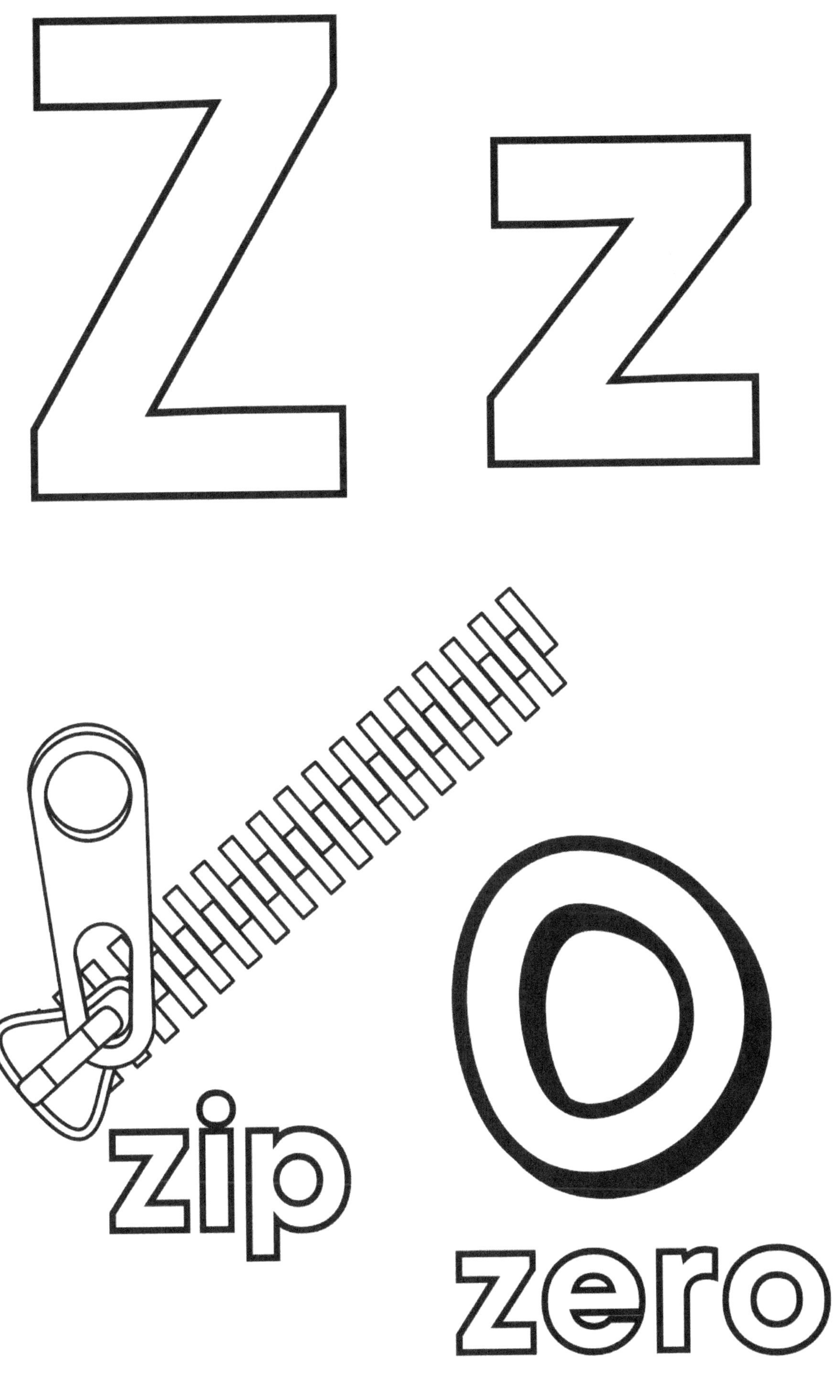
Z z
zip
zero

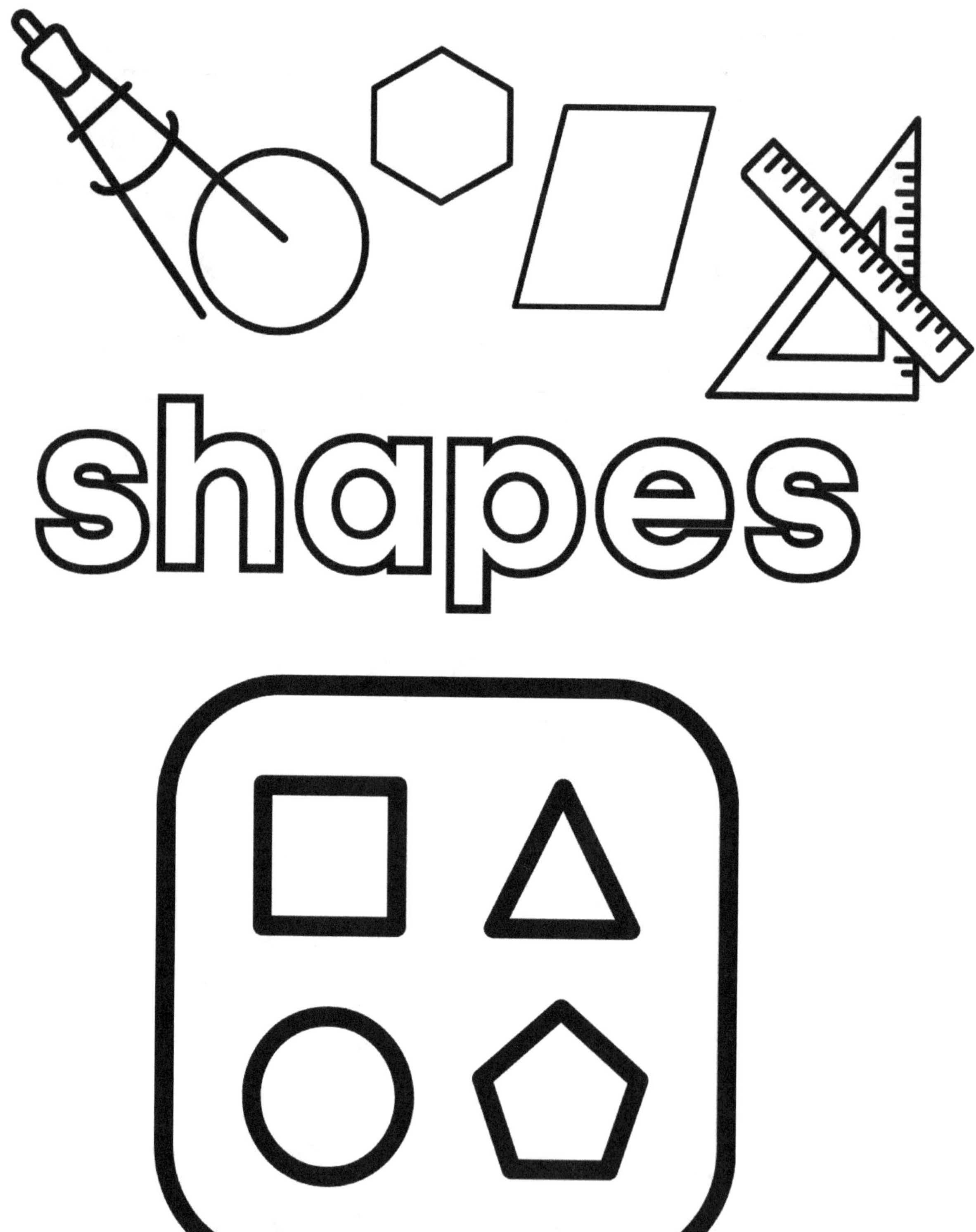

shapes

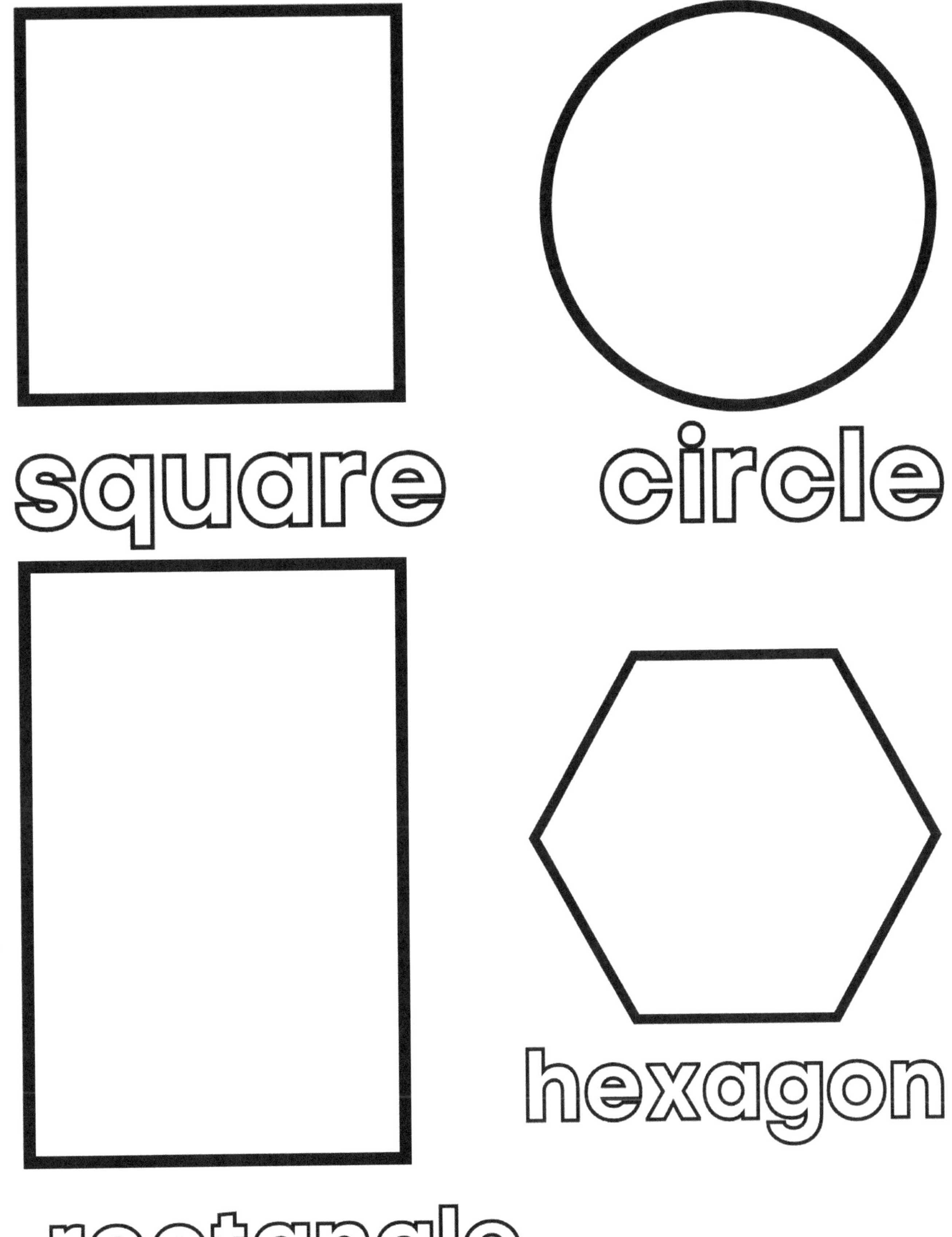

square
circle
rectangle
hexagon

heart
star
oval
triangle

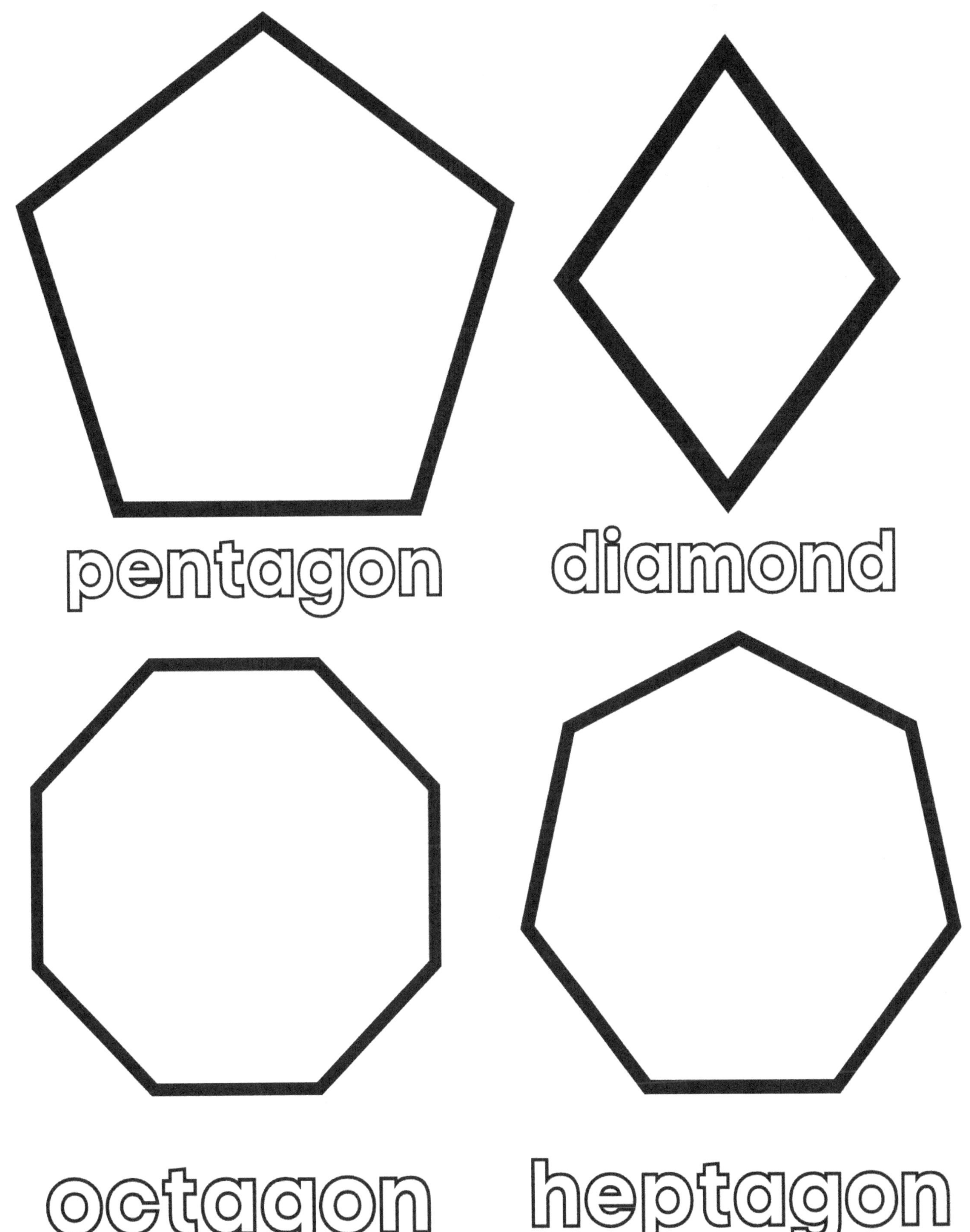

pentagon
diamond
octagon
heptagon

Colors

red

blue

green

orange

yellow
brown
pink
purple

white
black
grey

THE ZOO
ANIMALS

Lion
horse
Tortoise

Monkey
Elephant
Duck

Wolf
fox
Bear

a cow
Donkey
frog

Sheep
kangaroo
giraffe

Zebra

Koala

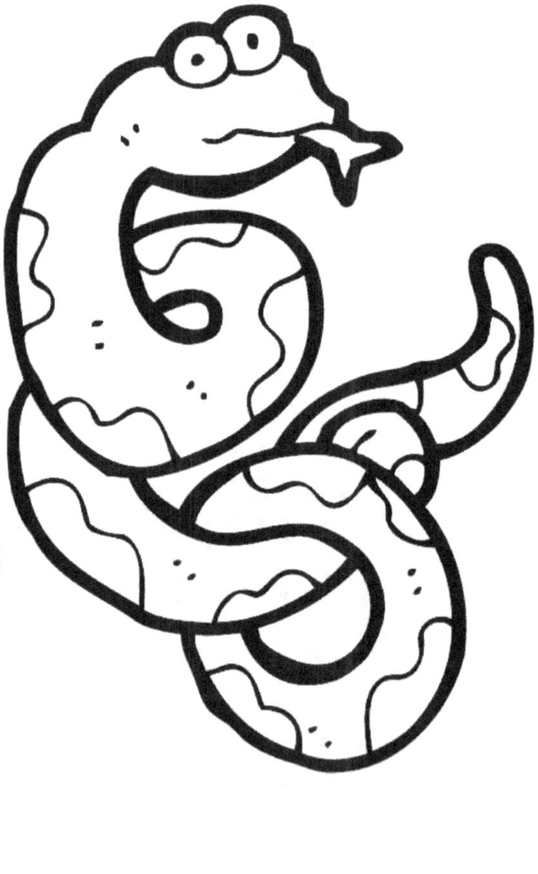

snake

Rabbit

Goose

dog

Cat

chicken

he-goat

crab

Fish

sea turtle

jellyfish

Balloon fish

whale

Octopus
sea Star
Dolphin

bird

Ladybird

Bee

butterfly

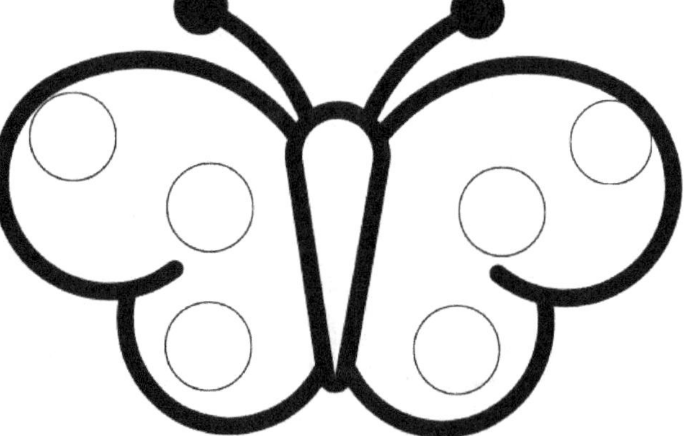

owl
Hedgehog
squirrel

ostrich
Buffalo
llama

Hyena

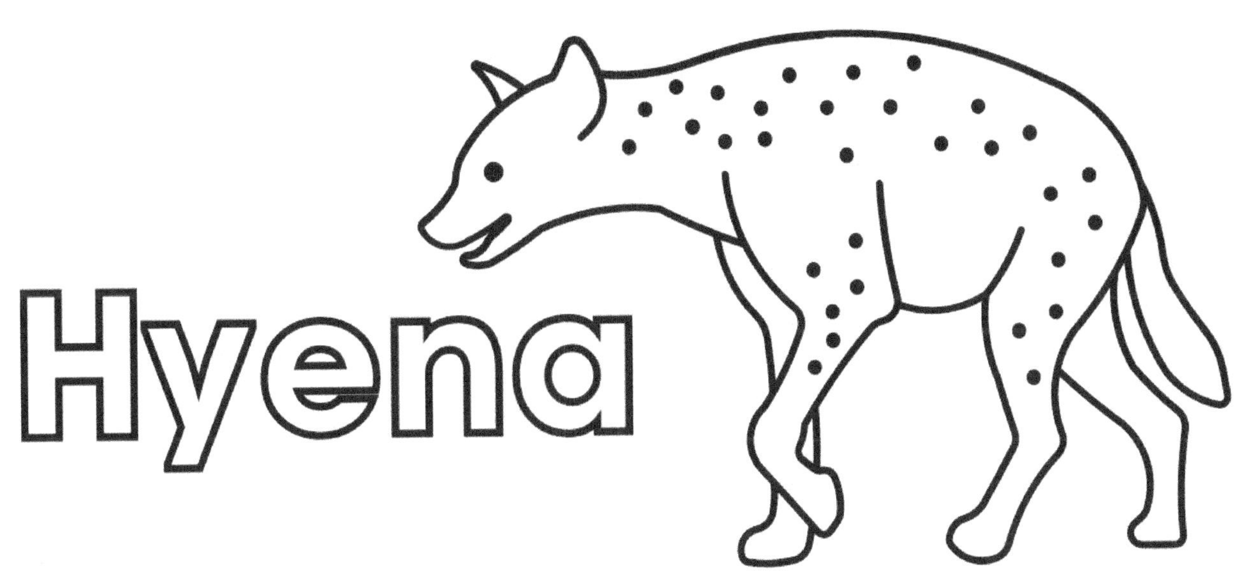

Armadillo

mongoose